ThickSkin

T0352475

PEAK STUFF

by Billie Collins

A ThickSkin Production. Commissioned by ThickSkin and Lawrence Batley Theatre. Supported by Shakespeare North Playhouse and Wigan Council. Winner of the New Play Commission Scheme.

Peak Stuff was first performed at Chichester Festival Theatre on 15 February 2024, before a tour of the UK.

by Billie Collins

Cast

Alice, Ben & Charlie	Meg Lewis
Musician	Matthew Churcher

Featuring voiceovers by Ajjaz Awad-Ibrahim, Esme Bayley, Matthew Churcher, Hetty Hodgson, Joe Layton, Vicki Manderson, James Westphal.

Director	Neil Bettles
Composers	Neil Bettles & Matthew Churcher
Video Design	Jim Dawson & Izzy Pye for TripleDotMakers
Lighting Design	Charly Dunford
Design	Neil Bettles
Associate Director	Hetty Hodgson
Sound Associate	Hannah Bracegirdle

Production Team

Production Manager	Tom Robbins
Touring Production Manager	Helen Morris
Lighting & Video Engineer	Sam Marshall
Scenic Construction	RT Scenic

For ThickSkin

Executive Producer	Laura Mallows
General Manager	George Soave
Production Administrator	Abi Beaven
Marketing	Make A Noise
Press	SM Publicity
Photography	Ray Chan

Supported by Arts Council England, Unity Theatre Trust and the Wigan Brighter Borough Fund.

The commissioning of *Peak Stuff* was enabled by a grant from the New Play Commission Scheme, a project set up by the Writers' Guild of Great Britain, UK Theatre and the Independent Theatre Council, and funded by Arts Council England, the Theatre Development Trust and donations from actors, directors, playwrights and producers.

With thanks to:
Emma Adams, Roya Amini, Becky Atkinson, Ollie Baines, Maeve Bolger, Lee Brennan, Tori Burgess, Kymberley Cochrane, Molly Crabtree, Mark Distin Webster, Andy Doyle, Steph Green, Neil Harris, Reuben Joseph, Tom Kelly, Matt Lever, Tom Mallows, Miriam, Siobhan Noble, Jonnie Riordan, Jack Sizzle, Andrew Smaje, Lane Stewart, Joseph Walsh, Liam Wilson, Charlotte Yeung, Access Creative College, HOME, Rose Bruford College North, Royal Exchange Theatre, The Lowry, The Old Courts and ThickSkin's Young Creatives.

Peak Stuff was originally developed with students from Pendleton College with support from The Lowry's Stage Directions Programme.

Cast

Meg Lewis | Alice, Ben & Charlie

Meg (they/she) trained at the Royal Welsh College of Music and Drama. Theatre credits include: *Tiger* (Omnibus Theatre); *Pitch* (November Theatre); *String* (Omnibus Theatre); *The Blue House* (Helikon Theatre Company); *Visits* (Clean Break/Papertrail); *The Lion's Den* (Camden People's Theatre); *Moon Licks* (Paines Plough); and *A Doll's House* (Sherman Theatre). For film & TV: *Achievement* (Tree Tops Films); *What We Doing* (London Film School); *Galwad* (Sky/National Theatre Wales); *Grey Mare* (Solent); *I Do Harm* (Newport Film School). Meg was awarded the Raymond Edwards Prize for their contribution to the arts in Wales. Their short play *A Disappointing Birthday Party* won Theatr Clwyd's Daniel Owens Writing Competition. Meg holds a British Sign Language Level 2 Certificate and is an associate artist of Helikon Theatre Company.

Matthew Churcher | Musician and Co-composer

Matthew (he/him) studied at the Royal Central School of Speech & Drama. He first performed with ThickSkin at the Olivier Awards in 2011. As a professional drummer/percussionist, Matthew has performed at the Royal Albert Hall (BBC), and toured internationally. Recently his band Citadel opened the BBC Introducing Stage at Latitude Festival. As an actor, his theatre credits include: *Gypsy, Brief Encounter*, *The Secret Garden* and *A Streetcar Named Desire* (all Pitlochry Festival Theatre); *Animal Farm* (Fiery Angel/Birmingham Rep); *Wolves In The Walls* (Little Angel Theatre); *Pippi Longstocking* (Royal & Derngate Theatre); *Peter Pan* (National Theatre/Bristol Old Vic); *White Teeth* (Kiln Theatre); *The Great Gatsby* (Theatre Clwyd/Square Chapel); *Jane Eyre* (National Theatre); *All or Nothing* (Rock and Roll Productions); *War Horse* (National Theatre and West End); *Ignition: 60 Hugs* (Frantic Assembly); *Loaded* (Out of Inc). Film credits: Ken Loach's *Star Wars* (Haiste & Lawrence); *Jamis Vu* (dir. Miguel Angelo Costa); *A Tragedy* (dir. Elisa Scubla); and *The Intruder* (dir. Leigh Lewis). Matthew has directed a number of productions, including Simon Stephens' *One Minute* at the Waterloo Vaults, which was nominated for 3 Off West End Awards.

Creative Team

Billie Collins | Writer

Billie (they/she) is a writer from the Wirral, based in Manchester. Their debut play *Too Much World at Once* was produced by Box of Tricks Theatre in Spring 2023. The play opened at HOME Manchester before touring nationally, and was published by Nick Hern Books. Other recent credits include: *Beltane* (RSC 37 Plays Project), two episodes of *Malory Towers*

Series 5 (King Bert Productions for CBBC) and and SAGA (BBC Radio 4). Billie was selected for the 2022 BBC Writersroom Northern Voices scheme, and also works as a script reader and dramaturg for organisations across stage and screen.

Peak Stuff by Billie Collins is the Winner of New Play Commission Scheme (Writers' Guild of Great Britain).

Neil Bettles | Director, Co-composer and Designer

Neil (he/him) is a director, choreographer and movement director. As co-founder and Artistic Director of ThickSkin his directing credits include: *How Not To Drown*, *Chalk Farm*, *The Static*, *Blackout*, *Boy Magnet* and *White Noise*, and for ThickSkin's Walk This Play series: *Keep Going Then Vanish*, *Your Time is Now* and *This Is Where We Begin*. Other directing credits: *The Unreturning*, *This Will All Be Gone* and *No Way Back* (Frantic Assembly). As Choreographer: *Assassins* (Chichester Festival Theatre); *Bedknobs and Broomsticks* (Disney). As Movement Director: *Great Expectations* (Royal Exchange Theatre); *James IV*, *Queen Of The Fight*, (Raw Materials/Capital Theatres); *Private Peaceful* (Jonathan Church Theatre Productions/ Nottingham Playhouse); *Carmen* (Opera Wuppertal, Germany); *The James Plays I, II and III* (National

Theatre of Scotland/Edinburgh International Festival/National Theatre); *Blood Wedding and The Bacchae* (Royal & Derngate). As Associate Movement Director: *Harry Potter and the Cursed Child* (Sonia Friedman Productions, worldwide); *Heisenberg* (Wyndhams Theatre); *The Light Princess* (National Theatre) and *The Full Monty* (Sheffield Theatres/West End). As Associate Director: *Disco Show* (La Mama, New York). Neil has received multiple awards for his work at ThickSkin.

Jim Dawson for TripleDotMakers | Video Design

Jim (he/him) is Creative Director of TripleDotMakers, specialising in mixing analog and digital technologies to achieve unique and innovative productions. Jim has directed and contributed to a wide variety of projects in film, television, theatre, audio-visual installations, commercials and music promos. For ThickSkin: *Petrichor* (an immersive VR film) and various short films for ThickSkin TV. Work with bands and recording artists: Elbow, Doves, James Morrison, The Verve, Editors, JP Cooper, Basil Clarke and Mr Scruff. As live VJ and animation producer: Mr Scruff (Ninja Tune). Jim has also worked with companies including Adidas, AND Festival, the BBC, English National Ballet, Factory International, HOME, Imperial War Museum, MEN Arena, National Football Museum,

The National Trust, People's History Museum, RHS Garden Bridgewater, Royal Exchange Theatre, The Shard London and Wembley Arena.

Izzy Pye for TripleDotMakers | Video Design

Izzy (she/her) trained at The Manchester Film School and is an independent filmmaker and creative, and a regular collaborator for TripleDotMakers. Her work as a director, writer and editor spans documentaries, short dramas, commercials, music videos and video design for live events. With TripleDotMakers, projects include work for: Adidas, The National Trust, The Lowry, The Harris and The Poverty Truth Commission. She won the Royal Television Society Award for Production Design in 2021 and the LA1 Shorts Audience Choice Award for the short film *Rose* in 2017.

Charly Dunford | Lighting Design

Charly (she/her) is a graduate from Liverpool Institute for Performing Arts. Lighting Design credits for ThickSkin include: *Driftwood* (Pentabus/ThickSkin) and *Blood Harmony.* Other theatre credits: *this is not a crime – this is just a play* (Liverpool Everyman); *Vagina Cake* (Hope Mill Theatre); *Silla* (Leeds Opera Festival); *Little Red Robin Hood* (Battersea Arts Centre); *Wild Swimming* (Full Rogue); *Séance* (The Station); *A Very Odd Birthday Party*

(Hawkseed Theatre) and *Much Ado About Nothing* (Shakespeare North Playhouse). Associate Lighting Design credits: *Curtain Up* (Theatr Clwyd); *Shades of Blue* (Matsena Productions); *The Sorcerer's Apprentice* (Northern Stage); and *STUFFED* (Ugly Bucket). As Assistant Lighting Designer: *Cabaret* (Kit Kat Club at the Playhouse); *What's New Pussycat* (Birmingham Rep). As Relighter: *Vortex* (Russell Maliphant Dance Company); *How Not to Drown* (ThickSkin/Traverse Theatre); *Shades of Blue* (Matsena Productions); and *Good Grief* (Ugly Bucket). Charly won the ALPD Michael Northern Award in 2023.

Hetty Hodgson | Associate Director

Hetty (they/she) is a theatre director who works collaboratively to tell stories which are both political and playful. They are the Artistic Director of multi-award winning Pigfoot, an associate company of English Touring Theatre, telling stories about the climate crisis with the least carbon impact possible. Directing credits for Pigfoot: *Hot In Here* (with Gate Theatre); *Bothered* and *How To Save A Rock* (with English Touring Theatre/Battersea Arts Centre's Let's Do London). Other directing credits: *I Really Do Think This Will Change Your Life* (Mercury Theatre); *Sharp* (LAMDA MishMash Festival). As Assistant Director: *GameChangers* (Megaverse); *Fanboy* (Worklight Theatre); *Miss Julie* (Elysium Theatre). Hetty is an experienced facilitator and has worked for: National Theatre, Southbank Centre, Guildhall School of Speech and Drama and HOME. Hetty's work has been shortlisted for The Stage Innovation Award.

Hannah Bracegirdle | Sound Associate

Hannah (she/her) trained at Bristol Old Vic Theatre School. Sound Design credits include: *Identities* (Close to Home Productions); *Burning Down the Horse* (Fishing for Chips); *Have a Break, Have a Kit Kat* (53two); *My Dear Aunty Nell* (Camden People's Theatre); *Conversations we've never had, with people we will never be* (Orange Moon Theatre); *Caligula and the Sea* (The Vaults) and *The Untitled Sparkly Vampire Play* (Teastain Theatre). Recent Technician credits: Sound Tech on *Debate: Baldwin Vs Buckley* (Bristol Old Vic) and *StageDoor Manor* (Performing Arts Theatre Camp); Sound No.2 on *The Jungle Book* (Chichester Festival Theatre) and *Wonderboy* (Bristol Old Vic); Duty Technician and Operator on *Four Seasons* (Little Bulb Theatre Company). TV credits include: Sound Trainee on Series 12 & 13 of *Waterloo Road* (BBC/Wall to Wall).

Tom Robbins | Production Manager

Tom (he/him) is a Production Manager working across physical and digital spaces to provide technical solutions that facilitate authentic storytelling. For ThickSkin credits include: *How Not To Drown* and *Blood Harmony.* Tom has recently worked with companies including National Theatre, Sheffield Theatres, Site Gallery, The University of Sheffield, Sheffield Hallam University, Common Wealth, Barrel Organ, Cement Fields, Pilot Theatre, Megaverse, RivelinCo, Andro & Eve, Paperfinch Theatre, Roots Mbili Theatre, Migration Matters Festival, Cambridge Literary Festival, Sheaf Poetry Festival, SICK! Festival, WOW! Festival, Estuary.

Laura Mallows | Executive Producer

Laura (she/her) is co-founder and Executive Director of ThickSkin. As Executive Producer for ThickSkin, productions include: *How Not To Drown*, *Blood Harmony*, *Walk This Play*, *Petrichor*, *Chalk Farm*, *The Static* and *Blackout*. Other credits include, as Producer: Survivor (Hofesh Schechter Company). As Associate Producer: *Beautiful Burnout* (Frantic Assembly/ National Theatre of Scotland). As General Manager: *Pool (no water), Stockholm* and *Othello* (all Frantic Assembly). Laura has also worked for Clean Break, Fifty Nine Productions, Manchester International Festival, Royal Opera House, Shobana Jeyasingh Dance, The Cholmondeleys and The Featherstonehaughs and the Touring Consortium. She is a trustee of Lawrence Batley Theatre and RTYDS.

Thick**Skin**

Extraordinary stories told in unexpected ways.

ThickSkin is reinventing theatre for the next generation. We are reimagining what theatre can be and looking to share human stories through quality, future-facing, multi-disciplined formats. We're developing 360° artists of the future for a hybrid world where physical and digital collide in more ways than ever before.

We produce bold and ambitious theatre; using our distinctive physicality and cinematic style to reach and inspire young, new and diverse audiences across the world. Our desire to make theatre accessible and exciting for young people underpins all our work. We draw on a wide range of creative approaches to tell stories in new and inspiring ways. From live stage productions to virtual reality experiences, to immersive audio plays, we make theatre that is rooted in contemporary culture.

ThickSkin has a long history of seeking out and supporting new talent, providing meaningful opportunities for collaboration alongside high-calibre creative teams. We nurture talented theatre makers, providing a springboard for artists who are ready to take a leap.

The company was founded by Neil Bettles and Laura Mallows in 2010 and quickly established itself as one of the UK's most exciting theatre companies, producing multi-award-winning productions, commissioning new writing and touring worldwide. The company joined the Arts Council England's National Portfolio in April 2023, with a new base in Wigan. Our activities will increase opportunities for young people in the borough, and for artists across the North through training and employment.

'All the ingredients to inspire a new generation in theatre.'
The Good Review

'That elusive new, fresh, and cool material you have been searching for.' *ManchesterTheatres.com*

For more information visit
thickskintheatre.co.uk

ThickSkin's work is generously supported by Arts Council England, Backstage Trust, John Ellerman Foundation, The New Play Commission Scheme, The Oglesby Charitable Trust, Unity Theatre Trust and Wigan Council's Brighter Borough Fund.

ThickSkin is the operating name of ThickSkin Theatre, a Registered Charity, no: 1188196 and ThickSkin Productions, a company limited by guarantee in England & Wales, no. 11568661. Studio 16 & 17, Gerrard Winstanley House, Crawford Street, Wigan, WN1 1NA.

Supported using public funding by
**ARTS COUNCIL
ENGLAND**

Rehearsal photos: performers Meg Lewis and Matthew Churcher; director Neil Bettles; associate director Hetty Hodgson.

Photography by Ray Chan

PEAK STUFF

Billie Collins

Writer's Note

'I'd like to have a revolution. But everybody's too busy
shopping.'   *Benjamin Zephaniah*

In Spring 2022, Neil and Laura asked me to write a play.
'Write us a play,' they said. 'Make it about consumerism.' (I'm
paraphrasing.) But Neil and Laura – I thought – surely the sorts
of people who write 'plays about consumerism' are the sorts of
people who know things about the economy and can do mental
maths? That's not me! I write plays about teenage crushes and
how much I like trees! I mean… *Consumerism?* That is a BIG!
VAGUE! CONCEPT! No way, dude. 'Consumerism' is too Big
and Vague and Conceptual a thing for me to write a play about.

So, I decided to write about 'stuff' instead. I started by making
lists of stuff I remember buying. Stuff I bought because I
thought it said something about me. Stuff I bought because I
was having a bad day. Stuff I regret buying. Stuff I totally *don't*
regret buying. Stuff I was worried about. Stuff I was angry
about. The need for more stuff, new stuff, better stuff. The
first pair of Dr. Martens. The last pack of chewing gum. The
euphoria and waste and comfort of it all.

I took all this stuff – all these lists and ideas and feelings – into
a workshop with Neil, some brilliant actors and a drumkit. It
was a big old experiment. But out of it, three voices started to
emerge. And out of *that,* over the course of a year and half, with
much trial and error (and lots of support from Neil and Laura)…
I wrote a play about consumerism.

Sort of.

                                                        B.C.

Terms and Conditions

Peak Stuff is designed to be performed by one ACTOR.

The ACTOR agrees to:

- Perform, to the best of their ability, dialogue ascribed to:
  - ALICE, *fifteen, school pupil*
  - CHARLIE, *twenty-five, unemployed*
  - BEN, *thirty-five, marketing associate*
- Keep up the pace.
- Not be boring.*

Additional User Guidance

- Dialogue in bold is not in the voice of ALICE, BEN or CHARLIE.
- Dialogue in italics is in real time, in the voice of ALICE, BEN or CHARLIE.
- Text in italics and within brackets are stage directions.
- 'Glitches' are disruptions to the flow. They may be images, sounds or movement. They might force leaps in time, place or perspective. They might be a sign of mounting system pressure. The key is not to drop the ball. Think about channel hopping. Think about switching tabs. Think: did I leave the oven on?

Small Print

*   'Not being boring' is the responsibility of the whole team (writer included).

This text went to press before the end of rehearsals and so may differ slightly from the play as performed.

(The audience enters. They take their seats. They'll probably faff around a bit.

Have they stopped? Good. Then let's begin.

The ACTOR *enters. It's time to choose your fighter! We cycle through three profiles…*

BEN

Thirty-five, marketing associate
Ben is six foot – not that it matters – and athletic
He needs glasses but refuses to wear them
And his interests include fitness, restaurants, vintage and mojitos.

Nope.

CHARLIE

Twenty-five, unemployed psychology graduate
Their Myers–Briggs personality type is INTP.
That is: Introverted, Intuitive, Thinking and Prospecting.
Charlie likes animated film and seventies disco
Shares a house with four strangers
And holds a five-hundred-day Wordle streak.

No thanks.

ALICE

Fifteen, secondary school student
Alice is in top set for maths, English and history
And is taking her French GCSE a year early.
She is a Pisces, never forgets to recycle, and can be found on
Snapchat, BeReal, Facebook, Instagram, TikTok and –

Bingo! Here we go!)

ALICE. I'm stood outside OOZIE.
    The branch of OOZIE that sits on the first floor
    Of the Manchester Arndale centre
    Next to Swarovski and opposite Levi's.

    If you don't know OOZIE, think Claire's Accessories
    But like... More.
    It's Friday afternoon, like two o'clock,
    And I'm about to do something terrible.

    I should be in school.
    I should be in double economics
    Drawing production possibility diagrams,
    But *this*... This is important.

    I go in, and inside smells like
    Cheap plastic and bubblegum.
    They've got strip lights and tinny speakers
    Playing Katy Perry on loop

    (ALICE *sings the first three lines of the chorus of Katy
    Perry's 'Roar'. She interrupts herself:*)

    Till on my right
    Piercing chair on my left
    And up ahead
    Just rows and rows and rows and rows
    Of earrings and rucksacks and nail stickers
    And fidget spinners and phone charms and popsockets
    And scrunchies and tiaras
    And all this *stuff*.
    And it's all sort of... Cheap.
    All sort of – y'know, tacky?
    And clean and disposable and neon
    And looking at it I start to feel a bit...
    The lights swim and my head aches
    Back sweating against my rucksack
    And I think I might...
    Stay focused.

I used to love OOZIE.
When I was twelve, my auntie gave me a tenner for Christmas
I came straight to this shop
And bought a holographic pencil case.
Sounds silly, but it was perfect.
Like, it was like *me* as a pencil case.
And that was the first time I'd ever...
My tenner, buying something *I* chose.

I smile at the shop assistant – friendly smile.
Count two CCTV cameras
One there, and one... There.
Do the kind of walk that says
'I'm not in a rush, but I did come here on purpose'
The walk I do when I'm buying condoms or in a museum.

I wait till she's distracted, piercing the ears
Of a little girl who's howling and stamping her feet
Trainers lit up like tiny ambulances
And to be honest, I want to run.
Cos what if I get caught?
Like, what if they call security, who'll call my parents
And I'll be arrested or suspended or sectioned
And I'll never have a job or a family or be happy
And the whole thing will be completely –

(*GLITCH!*)

STAY FOCUSED!

I crouch down behind some plushies –
Bulging eyes and button noses
Back to the cameras, little girl wailing
Open my rucksack and pull him out.

He lost a few feathers on the way.
And he stinks of fish, and salt, and death...
Because he is... Dead.
Wings broken, neck broken too
Little halo of fruit flies
And he's sort of... Small.
For a seagull.

I push aside the toys and sit him on the shelf.
Not hidden, but you'd have to – y'know, *look*.
And that's the point.
I think that's the… I'm not really sure.
But someone will.
Eventually.
Surprise.

CHARLIE. It's three twenty-two a.m.
My housemates are having a party downstairs
And I'm doing an online yoga class.
I'm not really into yoga
But I've been on my laptop all night
So I can't feel my legs.

I've been on ASOS
Filling my basket with things I can't afford
Putting in my card details
And clicking 'cancel transaction'
At the last… Possible… Second…

My room's tiny, so when I lie in shavasana
My head's under the desk
And the teacher's voice is disembodied
Like an angel or… Alexa.
She says:
Don't push yourself too far.
It's not a contest.
All you have to do
Is find the appropriate amount of sensation.

And if you asked me to identify the moment, this would be it.

Lying under my desk
In my damp-smelling room
Suddenly aware
Of every inch of my skin
The floor throbbing with
Muted laughter and muffled bass,
Trying, *really* trying to
'Find the appropriate amount of sensation' but…

(*A glitch. The bass swells.*)

Sometimes I feel like I'm not really here.
Then sometimes I feel like I'm *too* here,
Like my body is…

(CHARLIE *can't find the words*.)

And that's when the idea arrives
Fully formed, like when a giraffe gives birth.
Have you seen that? Google it, it's *awful* –
The idea arrives and it is *perfect*.

I pause the video and start with my finger
The pinky, on my left hand.
I figure I've got ten so I won't miss it too much.
I close ASOS and log on to www.etsy.co.uk.
Within ten minutes, I've made my first listing.
One finger, human, home-made.
Within twenty I have interest from seven different buyers.

BEN. The cocktail bar is underground,
    All pleather cushions and mirrored ceilings.
    The walls are plastered with legs, lips,
    Bodies, bodies, bodies –
    And a neon sign flashes 'PEEP SHOW' above the loo.

She picked the venue.

It's kitsch. Like, ironic, y'know?

Oh. Cool.

Her name's Miranda.
We met at work, and I know, *I know* –
But she's on secondment from Operations so
Different department, grey area,
And she made the first move.

Aesthetically, she's got this whole rockabilly goth thing
going on:
Victory rolls and a fat little cherub under her collarbone
Not my usual type, but one minute she's saying my Jordans
look tragic –

They don't –
The next I'm buying her a drink.

Dan's been texting.

The ex. Amazon delivery driver and chronic cheat.

Blocked his number.

Good for you.

Miranda's experience with Dan had two main consequences.
One, she finds it hard to trust people.
Two, she won't shop from Amazon in case he turns up.

You look amazing by the way.

Leopard-print corset, black-lace trim.

Not bad yourself.

Vintage Armani, Bleu de Chanel.

This is date number four.
We've covered veganism, rail strikes, true crime,
Three mojitos down, we're onto the big stuff.

What would you do if you won the lottery?

Retire early, move to Barbados. You?

I'd give it to my mum.

The way she says it, I really believe it.

(*His phone rings. He rejects the call.*)

D'you need to get that?

No. Sorry.

What's your mum like?

We're not close.

Why's that?

It's complicated… She isn't well.

But she loves you?

That's a tough question.

It's important to be loved.

You think?

Yeah. Makes you human.

She looks at me, then.
Bit tipsy, but she
Gives me this look, and smiles
The most brilliant smile, and it makes me feel…

(BEN *can't find the words.*)

We finish our drinks and head outside.

And it's a warm night.

Too warm, for the time of year.

Suddenly I have a bad feeling.
She says:

So.

And if you asked me to identify the moment, this would be it.
She's about to ruin everything.

Back to yours?

No can do, I'm afraid.

She looks surprised.

There was a fire in my kitchen last week.

Shit, really?

*Tumble dryer overheated. I called the company, I've not had
time to sort it, so –*

Back to mine, then?

Actually, should probably… Early start.

Alright, Granddad.

She kisses me.
Her lips taste like
Cigarettes and Cointreau
And I realise...
I like her.
I *really* like her.

And as she clip-clops away
I take out my phone
Block her number
And plan to hot desk from the fourth floor tomorrow.

ALICE. I'd been having nightmares.
Should've said that first, sorry –
The nightmares came before the seagull.
I was having nightmares cos of this video on TikTok...
I think I'm addicted to TikTok.
Like, sometimes I try and imagine what life would be like
without it
Like TikTok wasn't a thing when my parents were teenagers
Which must've been weird
Like people must've been really sure of themselves.
Cos to me, and I dunno, like, this is just me
But sometimes I feel like there's so much stuff to worry
about
I don't even know where to start.

Like every day I open my phone
And it's: genocide! Death toll! Platform boots!
And my mum says:

It's not real. Why don't you turn it off?

But she doesn't get it
Because it *is* real
And you can turn away or whatever,
But you can't really, cos it won't stop.

Anyway, I saw this video. Of some sofa cushions.
Big brown-leather sofa cushions.
And at first, I only glance it, so I think maybe it's an ad.
But then the cushions start moving.

Like heaving and squirming – smacking into each other
Because they're not cushions... They're walruses.
Huge walruses, arriving at their breeding ground,
Only the ice has melted so there isn't any room.
But they don't know what else to do so they just keep
coming.
They keep coming and coming,
Until they're piling up, all these bodies, and there's blood in
the snow...
And I'm watching this in form time, just after lunch.
Miss Wood calls my name, but I don't feel like I'm really
there.

I never thought about it before
But when something dies, it doesn't just disappear, does it?
It becomes like an object.
Like a thing.

Anyway, I started having nightmares.
Really gory, y'know, nightmares.
And I don't tell anyone,
Because well, it's weird, isn't it?
And there's people with like *real* problems.
Still, I wonder if anyone else ever feels...
Y'know, if anyone ever feels...

(ALICE *can't find the words*.)

And I think the only way I'm going to stop the nightmares
Is by doing something,
So I did.

Course the seagull was only a practice.
Like a test run.
'See if I had it in me' sort of thing.
Turns out I do, so...

BEN. A week later, Miranda goes back to Operations
So it's easier to avoid her at work.
Work, by the way, is a designer kitchenware company –
I'm in marketing.

I tell HR that Mum's illness has gotten worse
Not a lie, but I don't visit.
She went into hospital about a year ago –
Cancer, and other stuff.
Day she arrived, the nurse took her bag and said:
'Oh you've packed light.'
Mum said, 'well you can't take it with you.'

HR let me work from home
Except Fridays, when we have the Big Team Meeting
Inter-department, all-day thing, face to face.
Miranda will be there.
Which is… Fine.
Really, it's fine, because *everyone* will be there
And I have a presentation to do
So it's not like she'll have time to –

(*He collects himself.*)

I don't know if you've noticed, but ads have gotten shitter.
You can sit through two minutes of a skateboarding bulldog
singing 'Ave Maria'
Before you realise it's a pension provider.

Our current campaign is about reusable bags for supermarket
vegetables.
Kind of thing people buy to feel a little less powerless.
Fun fact: all bags are reusable.
If you reuse them.

So I'm in the Big Team Meeting
Pitching a stop-motion cartoon
About a very sorry seagull, when –

(*His phone rings. He rejects the call.*)

And this is a big deal for me.
Line Manager Rob is on paternity, so I've stepped in
And if I can impress the right –

(*Another call. He rejects it.*)

By the end of the PowerPoint, I have eight missed calls.
Eyebrows are raised, I keep it professional:

Any questions?

Miranda stands.

So, your phone *is* working then?

Someone sniggers.

I don't know what you mean.

She flushes red. Runs out the room.
Everyone goes back to their desks but
…I just can't, so
I follow her to the toilet –
Gender-neutral toilet, that sort of office –
Find her shut in a cubicle, sniffling behind the door.
I pass her some loo roll. She says:

Jess?

Jess is her best work mate… Do I have girly hands?

I really thought he liked me.

(*Pause.*)

And I want to say sorry.
I want to say it's not you, it's…
Or let's go for another drink?
But when she stands to leave
I duck into the next stall
Crouch on the toilet seat
And play Candy Crush
Till it's time to go home.

CHARLIE. From there, things take off faster than expected.
    The pinky goes like *that* so I move onto the next item
    And the next, and the next…
    In one week, I sell my hair, my toenails, my molars and pre-
    molars
    And the first two fingers on my right hand

Which makes it harder to work the microwave,
But I don't mind –
Because the woman in the post office has learned my name.

Back again, Charlie?

The packages must look weird,
So I tell her I have a small business
Selling monogrammed stationery –
Notebooks, pencil cases – *on Etsy, y'know?*
And she says:
That's very enterprising.
Though I suppose most young people have a – whatsit –
'Side hustle' these days, don't they?
I smile, pay for postage, and leave feeling… Lighter.

I haven't had a job in a while.
When I was at uni, I did casual hours
In Starbucks, Costa, and Premier Inn
And spent breaks being paid
To write fake product reviews
For all sorts of websites.
I would have imaginary feelings
About imaginary blenders
Air pods, electric guitars
Five stars all round
Nothing was better or faster
Or more reliable
Or more valuable
Than anything else.
And I liked that.
I enjoyed doing that.
But the truth is
I want to do something real.
I want to feel useful.
I would like to contribute,
And I do believe
I have things to offer.
I really do.

BEN. Five o'clock, I leave the toilet and head home.
I live in my mum's house.
Sounds sad, but it's a nice house;
Red-brick end-terrace up-and-coming area.
Not like she's using it.

There's a parcel on the front step.
Only ordered it yesterday –
It's mad how quick they deliver.
I take it through to the kitchen
Where I've got tonnes of freebies from work
Veg bags, a spiraliser, stuff Mum would *hate* –

(*His phone rings. He rejects the call.*)

She never liked having things.
Because the problem with having things
Is someone might take them away.
In fact, when I was a kid, there was only one thing –
One thing – she really cared about
One thing she really *loved*...
A little glass angel.
Tacky ornament
Gabriel probably. Peter? Who knows.
A gift from some priest or other
Used to sit on the mantelpiece,
And the light shining through it made
Rainbows on the wall.

Obviously, I wasn't allowed to touch it
So *obviously* I did.
I'd sneak down every night
And take it back to bed.
Don't ask why, kids do weird shit.
And this goes on for *years* without her knowing.
Only one night, I must've been about nine or ten...
I drop it.
Glass everywhere
Bloody footprints on the carpet
I'm crying, Mum comes down and...
Doesn't say anything.

I'm waiting for her to shout,
Shake me, smack me,
Part of me wants her to completely lose her rag –
But she doesn't.

Her hands tremble
And her jaw tightens
And something inside is gently folding inwards
And then just as fast…
She swallows it.
Hey presto.

She won't look at me.
Won't get me a plaster
Just sweeps up the angel
And puts it in the bin.
I say, 'I'm sorry Mum.'
Though I'm not, I say it anyway –
She says 'that'll teach you.
That'll teach you to look after things.'

(*His phone rings. Something grows inside him… He lets it ring.*)

There's a scorch mark above the tumble dryer.
Like a black hole, you could almost…

(*Maybe he goes to put his hand through it?*)

I open my parcel.

Box fresh running shoes.
Adidas running shoes.
A 3D-printed midsole, which –

(*His phone goes to voicemail.*)

Hi Ben. This is Dr Barton calling from Wythenshawe Hospital… Look, this isn't the kind of thing I like to do over the phone, it's just you haven't visited in a while, and I've been trying to call, but… I'm afraid your mum passed away last night. Around two o'clock.

(*Beat.*)

I'm sorry, Ben, but there's lots to be sorted out. Please call me back when –

(*BEEP.*)

Message deleted.

(BEN *clears his throat.*)

A 3D-printed midsole which minimises shin splints and –

(*Glitch! An image of some kind? Flesh? Sofa cushions? What IS that? Maybe it's growing?*)

And a grippy rubber outsole for traction on wet roads.
The *epitome* of stylish yet functional.
I take the shoebox to the living room
And stack it with the others.

(*He takes a second, inhales deeply.*)

You can't beat new trainer smell.
Leather, suede, rubber, and glue.
You just can't beat it.

CHARLIE. Having built a loyal and expanding customer base
I decide it's time to step up to some more... High value, high-risk items.
For example, my appendix.
I'm not using it, and the NHS website says
Appendectomy recovery takes a matter of weeks.
According to WebMD, the appendix is a small pouch,
Five to ten centimetres in length.
Some people think it's a vestigial organ
Which means an organ that has lost its primary ancestral function
Dictionary dot com says 'vestigial' comes from the Latin 'vestigium'
Which means footprint or trace.

I think lots of things will become vestigial in the not-too-distant future.

One appendix, human, home-made.
Listed, sold!
My gallbladder.
Listed, sold!
My left kidney.
Listed, sold!
Sold, sold, sold!
And so on, and so forth.

I have a routine now.
Every morning I organise deliveries,
And every evening I check my listings –
I don't even need to leave the house!
Tonight, the bidding war for my earlobes is gently fizzing
away,
I have two reviews from satisfied customers
And one new message:

**MURKYTURTLE77: I think what you're doing is
incredible.**

I click the profile.
No followers, no bio, no saved items, no nothing
But the profile pic… Is a still from *The Iron Giant*.
1999, Brad Bird's directorial debut.
It's one of my absolute favourite –

Uhh… Thanks?

**MURKYTURTLE77: I'd like to register interest in one of
your items.**

Which one?

**MURKYTURTLE77: It isn't listed yet, so sorry if this
seems presumptions.**

Presumptions?

MURKYTURTLE77: Presumptuous. Lol.

Lol.

MURKYTURTLE77: Are you taking advance bids on your brain?

(*Buffering. A pause as* CHARLIE *processes this.*)

MURKYTURTLE77: Hello?

My brain?

MURKYTURTLE77: Yes. Is it available for pre-order?

How much?

MURKYTURTLE77: However much you want.

Last year, my housemate got so far into her overdraft,
She tried to sell all her clothes on Depop.
Took ages cos she kept saying things like
'I wore this dress to my sister's wedding. It can't just go to anyone.'
In the end she gave up. Made an OnlyFans.

See, there are different kinds of value.
Something is only worth
What someone else is willing to pay
And I'm not a sentimental person but…

This is the dress I wore to my sister's wedding.
This is the stuffed rabbit my grandma gave me,
The shoes I wore to her funeral,
My ex's lighter, my father's fountain pen,
And *this* is the three-pound lump of fat and protein
I use to interpret and regulate every need, stimulus and experience –

(*Glitch.*)

MURKYTURTLE77: So…? Can I have it?

I don't know… It can't just go to anyone.

MURKYTURTLE77: So what do we do?

We keep talking.

ALICE. Because one branch of OOZIE isn't really…
    Like it's good, but it's not gonna *change* anything, y'know?
    And if you want to make a difference
    Like, if you want to make a *real* difference
    You have to go to the root.

    So I'm round the back of the OOZIE office HQ
    And I'm about to do something dangerous.
    There's like a two-hour window
    Between night shift and early security
    Where it's just the cleaner, and she works
    Headphones in, top floor down.

    I wait for her to take out the bins
    Leaving the door wide open so I can
    Sneak through the back, up the stairs
    To the third floor, find the Managing Director's office
    And get inside.

    It's easy.
    Like, TikTok said it would be easy.
    Hashtag Break and Enter.

    It's four-oh-six in the morning
    And even though the lights are off
    I can see hot-pink walls
    Plastic houseplants
    And countless crates
    Of surplus stock.

    I should be scared, but I'm not.
    Cos I've had a practice –
    The seagull, remember?
    And I've spent weeks planning
    When I should've been revising
    So now I can keep it
    Cucumber cool…

    I adjust my balaclava
    Spot one CCTV camera
    Spray-paint the lens
    And get to work.

This time, not a rucksack but a sports bag.
This time, not a seagull but
A whole seabass
A rainbow trout
A John Dory
Some sardines
Two cuttlefish
And the big one…
An octopus.

I had to save up.
I have a Saturday job in a café,
I'm not eighteen yet so I get five pounds an hour, cash in hand.
Dad said having a job would teach me some responsibility.
Would teach me the *value* of things.
Fishmonger thought I was nuts.

I work fast, arranging sea creatures on the desk,
The wheelie chair, the wastepaper bin.
I drape the octopus over a mannequin –
All fleshy, grey, and limp
Like a prop from a bad horror film.
D'you know octopuses have nine brains?
We learned that in biology.
Our nervous system is like – dead centralised,
But theirs is sort of spread out,
Like it's not just *one thing* doing the thinking
They see the world completely differently,
And they feel in ways we could never –

(*The lights come on. An alarm sounds.*)

Shit. I grab my bag and take one last look…
Looks like a crime scene.
And in a few hours' time, the *smell* –
Salt and sea and death –
Will be like… *Rank*.
And that'll teach them, won't it?
That'll teach them the value of things.

BEN. Ten days after The Event,
  I find myself in a shitty multi-use community centre.
  Kind of place that does book clubs and sit-down yoga.
  Chris from the Charity ushers me into a small room
  He looks like a children's-TV presenter...
  Floppy hair and fun socks.

  We were supposed to meet weeks ago:
  After the tumble-dryer incident
  Before my date with Miranda.
  But things got kind of busy,
  Y'know life gets in the way?
  And I might've just forgot...
  Sort of... Accidentally-on-purpose.

  He sits me down and makes me a cuppa
  Really shit cuppa by the way, and says –

It's good to see you, Ben.

I say, *is it?*

He says –

You never returned my calls.

I've been busy. Family stuff.

And this 'family stuff', it prompted you to reach out?

No. I'm here because I have to be.

Is that right?

I was referred by the fire service. They said I had to attend.

You don't *have* to do anything. You chose to be here, Ben.

Sure.

So. How are you?

Yesterday, I told HR that Mum is...
That I need compassionate leave.
Not a lie, but I don't claim the body.
And even though I've blocked her

Miranda has made new profiles
On Facebook, X, Instagram
And maxed out my DMs asking
Who do I think I am?

Fine. I'm fine.

He leans back in his chair.

Have you ever noticed your house smell?

My what?

Y'know? Your house smell? When someone comes to your house and says, 'oh it smells like you' and you think, a) what do I smell like? And b) why are you smelling me?

He pauses. Like I'm meant to laugh.

The trouble is, Ben, most people don't notice their normal.

When I was a kid, our house smelt like disinfectant. Like a crime scene.

In fact, it's very difficult to look at any situation objectively when you're inside it.

But that's how she liked it; cleanliness, godliness, et cetera.
Mum used to say you could be visited at any time,
And any visitor could be an angel in disguise.
He says –

Now then, let's have a look at this.

Like I'm a toddler, struggling with phonics.

It's called the Clutter Image Rating.

He produces a series of nine pictures.
The same room, nine times.
Image one is peak Marie Kondo.
Two's a couple mugs on the side
By five you've got boxes up the wall
And at nine you can't get in the room.
He says:

Which of these images looks most like your lounge?

Which fucks me off because who says 'lounge', it's a *living room*.
And I know the right answer.
I know the cheat code to make this all go away.
I know that all I have to do is –

(*GLITCH – a series of nine images. Blink-and-you-miss-it.* BEN *finds himself pointing.*)

Number seven?

No, sorry, I mean –

It's okay, Ben.

And Chris from the Charity smiles
Like he's – I dunno, eaten a baby.
And he talks…
About cycles and therapies and proactivity
About how *recognising you have a problem*
Is the very first step
And I feel…
Like a black hole.
Like my edges are going to dissolve
And everything's going to spill out.

I like having things.
I like having lots of things.
It makes me feel…
It reminds me that I'm, y'know –
A *person*.

My shit tea has gone cold.

I'd like to set you a challenge.
This week, I want you to dispose of one item.
Just one.
And I want you to *notice* how that feels.
Okay?

CHARLIE. We get closer, me and my friend.
　　Questions about pricing and delivery

Become questions about my day,
My favourite food, last night's sleep.
We send each other things.
Our love language is internet detritus,
Data scrap, the online equivalent
Of finding a tenner in an old pair of jeans.
He sends me a gif of a biblically accurate angel,
I send him a two-hour loop of Jeff Goldblum laughing in
Jurassic Park.
We talk every night, late into the night.
But only sometimes do we talk about –

MURKYTURTLE77: Made up your mind?

About what?

MURKYTURTLE77: Selling it to me.

Not yet. I need to know you'll look after it. Properly.

And then the conversation returns to
J.K. Rowling, conspiracy theories
The way things are bad and getting worse all the time.
And all the while business is booming.
I personalise the items –
Offering a gift-wrapped option,
A chocolate truffle in every box.
I promise quality and I deliver –
Which means going to bed early
Eight hours every night
I stop eating processed food
Drink two litres of water every day and I feel –

Good. Like I have a purpose.

MURKYTURTLE77: A destiny?

A reason. To look after myself.

MURKYTURTLE77: That's bleak. You're a human being, not a product.

Sounds like a Nike ad.

(*Beat.*)

MURKYTURTLE77: Can I tell you something?

Anything.

MURKYTURTLE77: Sometimes I feel like I'm not really here.

(*This stops* CHARLIE *in their tracks.*)

Me too.

MURKYTURTLE77: Like I'm drifting… Like it's all too much and I might just disappear.

Like you can't find the appropriate amount of sensation?

MURKYTURTLE77: Yes!!!!

Like there's a feeling and you can't describe it, but maybe if you could then…

MURKYTURTLE77: People would understand.

I send him a link. My favourite song.
Then log off and get ready for bed.
And even though I've sold my teeth to a man in Texas,
My tongue to a woman in the Netherlands,
My soft palate to a mother of three,
Throwing in my lips as a two-for-one deal –
I go to sleep with a smile on what's left of my face.

(*MURKYTURTLE77 clicks the link: 'You Make Me Feel (Mighty Real)' by Sylvester.*)

ALICE. **You're letting yourself down.**

This is Mum, over dinner.
We eat with the telly on
Veggie lasagne and garlic bread.
My mock exams are days away,
I've failed every practice paper,
And she is really worried.
Which like, I *get*…
But surely the mock *is* the practice paper?

Like at what point does the real test start anyway?
Cos it's not like I'm lazy I've just been... Distracted.

I keep checking my phone.
I search OOZIE OFFICE FISH
DEAD SEAGULL MANCHESTER
But nothing comes up.
I mean loads, *loads* comes up,
But nothing relevant:
Seagull dead stole my sandwich, men ain't shit.
Seagulls beat Man U 3-1 at Old Trafford.
Reheating fish in the office microwave should be illegal!
And I'm worried I've been wasting my time.
Worried it's all been for nothing.
And I'm starting to think about
Like, not just OOZIE
But Boohoo and Nasty Gal
And SHEIN and Missguided
And bodycon dresses
And two-pound T-shirts
And crotchless pants
And about how it's all – y'know, flammable?
Like it's all 95% polyester, 5% elastane
And it's all gonna become
Illegal landfill in the Atacama Desert
Where it will stay for like two hundred years
Way outlasting us.
I mean think about it –
One day, we will all be dead,
All this will be gone
And there will be nothing left except
Crotchless pants at the end of the world.

It's not like you.

Says Dad, mouth full, like he knows what I'm usually like.

In future –

They're particularly worried about the future.

**In future, if you want people to take you seriously, you
have to work hard.**

I think about telling the truth.
That I can't focus on AQA when I know time is running out
But I'm not sure how to say the crotchless-pants thing
In a way they'd understand.
So I just eat my lasagne
And stare at the TV
Where a news reporter is saying:

**The Managing Director of accessories brand OOZIE
announced his resignation this morning.**

Wait – turn it up?

**Martin Waterford's departure from the Mancunian 'fast
fashion' giant feels particularly significant in light of the
city's upcoming regional climate conference.**

Cut to: a man in a suit
Scurrying out the same office
I left like fifteen hours before.
And it's only quick
But you can sort of see it.
He looks scared.
Like he's come back to himself
Like he's realised the sofa cushions
Aren't *actually* sofa cushions and –

**He cited a managerial mental-health crisis in a statement
to colleagues earlier this morning –**

And maybe this sounds mean
But that makes me feel good.
Because that was *me*. I did that.
And it's like a weight has been lifted.
Like *now* you understand
And everything's shiny
Like a holographic pencil case and –

**He declined to comment, however, on a factory fire that
broke out in Bangladesh last week.**

(ALICE *stops…*)

The screen glows orange and red.

Twelve women died in the blaze and many more were injured –

Cut to: crying and flashing lights.

The factory in question failed numerous health and safety checks –

Cut to: hard hats and rescue efforts.

And as OOZIE was its primary client, there's much speculation as to the *real* reasons for Waterford's resignation.

I take out my phone
Check TikTok, Insta, BBC News
Read and reread the story
Until the truth sinks in.
And the truth is –

(*Glitch! Fire? Fish scales? Something shiny? Holographic?*)

He didn't go because of me.
I haven't changed anything.
I am fifteen years old.
I don't even have my GCSEs.
Who do I think I am?

An investigation follows
And no one is held accountable
He resigns, but there's no punishment
Women burned to death
For like thirty pee an hour
And there's that feeling again…
Like maybe I should just give up, but…

I've always been conscientious.
Teachers call me 'conscientious'.
Like, life isn't meant to be easy
That's what they say, isn't it?

Life shouldn't just be easy the whole time.
And if the fish weren't enough
And if they didn't notice me before
And if I want someone to get it
If I *really* want them to get it, then –

Are you listening? Are you even listening to me?

Yes. Yes, Dad. I am listening.
More than that.
I'm planning my next move.

BEN. A dressing gown.
Mum's, Lilac, ASDA George...
I find it in the attic with other stuff
She never cared about
Bring it downstairs and stand in the hall.

Dressing gown in one hand
Bin bag in the other
I play chicken.
Go on then.
One item.
And *notice* how it feels...

(*A shudder of a glitch. A pause as* BEN *holds it down.*)

Sometimes, Mum saw things that weren't there.
Angels in the living room...
She believed we are at the mercy of forces
Far beyond our understanding.
Like... Subbuteo players
Knocked about the cosmos
By God's divine hand...

My fingers tighten around the fabric
I think: I will never see her again.
I think she is dead and I do not miss her.
I keep thinking it, until it becomes something solid
Something I can swallow or put through a window.
I make my own decisions
I'm not doing this for Chris,

I'm doing this because *I* want to.
Because I don't need it
Because she doesn't live here any more
Because it's not about the dressing gown
Jesus Christ, I *know* it's not about the sodding dressing gown
So I can do one item.
I could do six
If I wanted.
Go on then.
One item, and *notice* how it –

Hello?

There's a knock at the door.

Ben?

Miranda?

Rob gave me your address.

Shit.

I can see you.

She kneels.

I can see the shape of you through the glass.

The letterbox frames her lips.

You ghosted me.

I stay completely still.

You can't treat people like they're worthless.

I count the shoeboxes, floor to ceiling.

It isn't *human*, Ben.

Adidas, Nike, Puma –

And I'm worried. I'm worried about you.

New Balance, Nike, Reebok –

No one's seen you at work. I don't think you're very okay, are you?

Converse, Nike, Lacoste –

Can we talk, Ben? I want to help.

I hold my breath.
She knocks again, sending an avalanche of fresh kicks
Crashing down the hall.
I count her steps as she clip-clops away
Exhale, pick up the boxes
And restack them
This time, in front of the door
Like Tetris, no gaps.

I drop the dressing gown.
Put down the bin bag.
Go through to the living room
Open my laptop
And spend one thousand seven hundred pounds
On an Echelon Stride folding treadmill.

I do this because Chris from the Charity is wrong
Miranda is wrong
Everyone is wrong
I have friends
I am well dressed
Comfortable in my masculinity
And good at my job.
I *contribute*
I don't *have* problems.
No more than anyone else.
Because don't you?
When you feel sad
Or powerless
Or lonely
Or bored
Or literally anything for once in your life,
Don't you?
Buy shit?

CHARLIE. So it continues
    And we're onto the big ones

The vital organs
The liver goes to an alcoholic
Four years down the wait list and –

BEN. It continues.
The treadmill is followed by a Peloton
A cross trainer
Retail therapy, they call it,
Fucking works.

CHARLIE. It continues.
The spleen to a medical student on the other side of the world
Who can't stand the sight of blood any more;
It makes him sick –

BEN. It continues
The gas card runs out
But I don't top it up.
Instead, I buy a drum kit
A bass guitar
A saxophone
I fill the house with noise.

CHARLIE. It continues
The stomach, the bladder, the kneecaps
And all the while we keep talking.
And no matter how much of me goes
He is still there
And I am still here
I am needed, I am useful
And I can trust that
I can know it.

BEN. It continues
Until my mum's red-brick end-terrace is fit to burst
And with next-day delivery
It only takes a week
To jump from the seventh picture to the ninth
And the thing is
It's all treasure
That's the thing, yes!

It's *all* treasure.
And what world to live in
Where nothing is better
Or faster
Or more useful
Or more real
Than anything else.
I think she's gone
And this is my house now.
I keep thinking it
Until it becomes something sticky, like Polyfilla
And I can use it to stuff the cracks in the skirting board and –

CHARLIE. It continues
And we share things
Me and my friend –
We imagine a world without limits
Where stuff doesn't end but accumulates
Where there is room for everyone and everything
And it doesn't matter how big our ideas get
Because he is my North Star
And I have never felt so close to another person
In my whole entire –

BEN. It continues
I stop working altogether
And with no money coming in
I take out a payday loan
And use it to buy
A pair of brass cufflinks
A crystal decanter
A virtual reality headset
And wish she hadn't said
So.
Which she hadn't said
Back to yours?
And ruined everything
With her cigarettes and Cointreau
Little collarbone cherub

It's important to be loved
I let my voicemail fill with –

**Hiya mate, it's Chris. We had another appointment
scheduled, I wondered how you were getting on with –**

Every blank minute with –

Failure to pay by the date previously mentioned –

And –

**Good morning, this is Siobhan from Got2Go Waste UK.
Do you have two minutes to talk about –**

CHARLIE. The heart to a woman
Who once worked with Mum.
Who says I came up on Facebook
And only meant to say hello
But she saw I had a business
And thought why not buy –

BEN. A pair of tweezers.
A deck of Silver Jubilee commemorative playing cards.
A home blood-pressure kit.
A beginner's guide to CBT.
A blue plush slanket in XXL.
A Sylvanian Families Shoe Boutique.
A bread maker.
A forty-three-inch Samsung Smart TV.
A rape alarm.
A yoga mat.
A Limited-Edition Talking Heads vinyl.
A 2012 Olympic Mascot Toy.
An X-Box 360.
A GameCube.
A pack of condoms.
A three-seat leather sofa from DFS.
A BB gun.
A holographic pencil case.
A day to a page spiral-bound diary.
A Chilly's reusable water bottle.

A lint roller.
A Rubik's cube.
An air fryer.
A Kinderkraft two-in-one pram.
A Mulberry Heritage holdall from Selfridges.
An eight-pack of Oral-B precision clean toothbrush heads.
Richard Osman's latest crime novel.
And a fish tank.
And a pasta machine.
And *The Complete Works of William Shakespear*e.
And a Watermelon Ice e-cigarette.
And it continues
And it continues
And it continues
Until –

CHARLIE. I'm barely there.
I have sold off every organ, bone, limb and extremity
On www.etsy.co.uk
And with one thing left I've made up my mind.
Five twenty-six a.m.
In my too-small room with the sun peeking out
Fanta orange and purple like a bruise
I log on.

MURKYTURTLE77: Hello.

You can have it.

MURKYTURTLE77: Are you sure?

It has to be you.

And you might wonder,
Why the brain?
Why make such a song and dance about the –
Why not the heart?
The heart is plumbing.
The brain is wetware,
Limitless, a man-made miracle,
And I'm willing to be sentimental on this one.

Promise you'll look after it?

MURKYTURTLE77: I promise.

I've made a listing.

RESERVED: one brain, human, home-made.

So. Name your price.

I hold the air in what would be my lungs
And squeeze what would be my nails
Into the ghost flesh of my palm.
I stare at the screen
And wait...

And wait…

He doesn't reply.
For what feels like hours.
I think I might explode but then –

MURKYTURTLE77: Why are you doing this?

What do you mean?

MURKYTURTLE77: You don't need money, do you?

Everyone needs money.

MURKYTURTLE77: But that's not why you're doing this.

No.

MURKYTURTLE77: So why are you doing this?

Because I stopped going out and no one noticed.
Because nothing feels real these days anyway.
Because I thought if I made there be less of me, I would be more.
Because there is no 'appropriate' amount of sensation
There is just a feeling, and it's so big it *frightens* me, but –

I want to know.

MURKYTURTLE77: Know what?

How much I'm worth.

(Pause.)

MURKYTURTLE77: I think we should meet IRL.

I thought you were impressed.

MURKYTURTLE77: I like you.

I like you too.

MURKYTURTLE77: So things could be different. We could be close.

And what's left of me shudders.
The remaining atoms vibrate
With thoughts of –

MURKYTURTLE77: What do you think?

(Pause.)

I must take too long to reply
Because that's when he sends it.
Drops it in my inbox
Like a discarded tissue.
And it's hard to make out at first
It's blurry.
And I think… Is it?
Of course, it is.
It was always going to be…
A picture of his penis.
Flaccid, taken from below
Dimly lit with a patch of stomach
Fuzzy in the corner.
He leaves it there.
And all I can think is…
Funny.
Not funny ha-ha
But funny
To see an organ like that
Detached
Floating in the data stream

Another thing to look at
Something else to think about
'Funny' is the first thing I think.
The second is –

Fuck you.

MURKYTURTLE77: Oh, come on. Don't play games.

This isn't a game.

MURKYTURTLE77: Isn't it? 'Selling your brain?' Your whole body? You're just sending pictures, right? NFTs or something.

No, I –

MURKYTURTLE77: It's okay. We both know it's made up. It's… idk. Performance art.

It's real.

MURKYTURTLE77: Then how are you typing? How are we talking?

I trusted you.

MURKYTURTLE77: You wanted attention. I gave you attention. I thought we understood each other.

So did I…

MURKYTURTLE77: So go on then. Your turn.

(*A catastrophic GLITCHHHH!*)

ALICE. Today's the day. My first mock GCSE exam –
Maths paper one, no calculator.
In ten minutes, everyone will file into the gym
And turn over their answer sheets…
But not me.
I'm in Albert Square.

(*Beat.*)

Not like *EastEnders* Albert Square
I mean the *real* Albert Square

Albert Square *in Manchester*
It's Friday morning, like eleven o'clock.
And I'm about to do something impossible.

There's a booming in my chest;
Like, I can *feel* the drums before I see them,
And the air is thick with sirens and shouting
Protesters and reporters
Swarming the steps of the town hall
With this big banner draped over the door:
'NORTHWEST REGIONAL CLIMATE CONFERENCE'.
A riot of noise and colour
Like TikTok, but real and close,
And suddenly, above it all:

Look! Look at the girl!

Pointing and shouting –

Do you see that? What *is* that?

And people don't turn at first.
But then the voice is joined by another –

Look! The girl! What's she doing?

And all it takes, is one person
Then two, then three –
The look spreads like wildfire
And all of them
Turn and stop and notice
Me.
Dragging a cow up to the door
Gripping its hind legs in both hands
Fur matted with mud and chewing gum –

Is it real?

It can't be real.

It's too heavy.

***Way* too heavy for –**

What is she? Fourteen?

I reach the edge of the crowd and
People start filming
Reporters push to the front:

What's your name?

Where are your parents?

Did you kill it?

Who sent you?

Is it meant to be some sort of... Statement?

I climb the steps, one at a time
The cow's head smacking on stone
It's almost too big for the door
So I give it a one... Two... Three!
Shove – and it rolls inside.
And maybe it's the look on my face
Or the smell of rotting flesh
Or the feat of impossible strength
But no one tries to stop me
No one dares.

The town hall is packed
With politicians and scientists
Minor celebs and journalists
And all of them, every one
Does absolutely nothing
Except crane their necks and gawk at me
Dragging a cow almost twenty times my weight
Towards a podium
Where the keynote speaker is clearing his throat.
And with one final *heave*
I'm there.

The protesters spill in from outside
And the crowd looks at me, wide eyed and hungry
Like they think I'm gonna say something.
Like Greta Thunberg about to make a big inspirational
speech
About our house being on fire

About my generation being dealt a shitty hand
About the bees dying and deforestation
About this being *your* mess
So *you* better clean it up
About how owning things
Means you need to take responsibility for them
About the endless, mindless, careless consumption
Of people and animals and resources and
Stuff.

But I dunno if I even *believe* any of that.
I don't know what I think about anything any more.
I just want someone to get it, this feeling.
And if *anyone* is going to get it,
It must be someone here, right?

There's a horrible pause.
Where we all stand together.
Staring at it.
This thing.
In a place where it shouldn't be.
Where there's no room for it.
And if you asked me to identify the moment
This would be it.

The keynote speaker, white as a sheet
Nudges the cow with his foot
And smiles
A friendly smile
An *everything's okay* sort of smile
And says:

Don't worry, everyone.

It's not real.

It's just a statement, that's all.

It's not real.

And everyone sighs
A *thank fuck for that,* sort of sigh
As I look down the camera

Straight down the lens
Before a policeman enters
Takes hold of my wrist
And escorts me outside, where –

(*Glitch – the sky is falling!*)

CHARLIE. I block my friend and delete my Etsy account.
At first, I'm bitter.
I think 'this is why people can't have nice things'.
I've gone to all this trouble,
And all I have to show for it is a figure.
A number.
I know *how much*.

Thing is, numbers are made up
And even then, I could've gotten more.
Probably could have haggled a bit.
But what can you do?
Besides. What would I spend it on?
Clothes? Swimming lessons?
Of course, the figure doesn't include the brain.
Which is still there.
Doing all the stuff brains do.

I sit in a room that isn't even mine.
The furniture belongs to a man I've never met.
And with the realisation that my friend can't be trusted
That he won't look after it, not like I asked him to
Comes the realisation that no one person can be trusted.
And you can't control that.

Sometimes I feel like I'm not really here
And that might be alright
If it weren't so lonely…

And with an immense, miraculous, invisible effort
The brain resolves these thoughts like pixels
Into one Great Big Thought, which is…

If you can't beat them…

So. I put on my favourite song.

(*Perhaps we hear Sylvester, somewhere far away…*)

And I give it away.
For free.
Open source.
On the internet.
The centre of my consciousness
Everything I am
The wetware
The grey matter
The good stuff
I give it away
Oprah style
To as many people as I can.
You get some brain!
And you get some brain!
And YOU get some brain!

(*Perhaps the sound of sirens, bleeding in through the music…*)

I give everyone a piece of my mind.
And they download it hungrily.
Take it all in.
Rewrite and replicate and share.
I explode myself in countless directions
Seeking home in every corner of the earth
I slip through the cracks
Tentacles reaching out over and over
Hoping for something to hold onto.
Billions of faces bathed in blue light –
I evaporate into data, into code,
Into whatever angels are made of
Iridescent and holographic
Owning nothing
And owned by no one until
It's not just one thing doing the thinking
There's no difference between me
And everything else
Like all the different parts of me are talking to each other

And the *sensation* is like nothing I've ever felt before
All these connections
All this energy
Lighting me up
And if you asked me to identify the moment
I couldn't.
There is no single moment
No cause and effect
Just a never-ending vortex of stuff
And all of it
Absolutely *all of it,*
Every last bit
Is important.

It all matters.
And hey presto.
Just like that…

BEN. The house is completely full.
Floor to ceiling, wall to wall.
There's just about room
To stand in the kitchen
Arms by my sides.
I'd only have to sneeze
And the whole thing would collapse.
So I stay stock still.
And when I close my eyes
I can see shapes, patterns,
Drifting swirls of colour.

There is not a sound –
But the whisper of breath
And if I listen really, *really* closely…
My heart…
Drumming away.

I'm completely surrounded.
There's no way out,
And no way in.
And some people might find that claustrophobic,
But not me.

Anything could be happening out there.
Storms, wars, plagues
Miranda from Operations
The Big Team meeting
Terrible fucking adverts
Any awful thing could be raging away,
And I wouldn't know.
Because all that matters is solid.
All that matters is here.
I know where everything is.
You can ask me,
I know where every single thing is.
And it isn't going to move
And neither am I.
As Mum would say
A place for everything
And everything in its place.

I think: I miss her.
I love her and I hate her and I miss her and I do not want to
be alone...
I keep thinking it.

I stand there for three days
Until the tingling in my ankles
Crackles up to my calves
My stomach
The very tips of my fingers
The numbness becomes pleasant,
And that's when I hear it...
Music.
Full cheese seventies disco
Bleeding through from next door...

And out the corner of my eye
In the lounge, *living room* –
Whatever you want to call it.
On the mantelpiece.
Fuck.
On the mantelpiece, there's...

A glass angel.
Intact.
I'm not lying.
Gabriel, Peter, whoever –
I *broke* you, you smashed...
Sat on the mantelpiece.
Like a joke. Back again? Hey?
And I can't move
So I can't touch it
I can't check if it –

(BEN *laughs*.)

The music gets louder.
An angel in the living room, and I feel...
Lighter...
And then the plastic casing of a copper wire
Behind the oven cracks
Under the weight of the stuff on top
And the spark
Becomes an ember
Then a flame
And I didn't think there was *space*
But the room fills with smoke
And the whole thing catches.
But it's okay.
Because I can *whoosh* straight into it.
I'm not kidding
I let my edges dissolve and
Whoosh out of my body
And into the angel
And the light of me
Refracts and chucks rainbows
In all directions
I'm not fucking with you
This is *real*
The blaze grows, furious and brilliant
But it doesn't touch me
Because I'm already gone

I'm gone already –
Bursting through the cracks and –

(BEN *sings – 'You Make Me Feel (Mighty Real)' by Sylvester
– the sound reaches a climax before… Silence? Emptiness?
Stillness? A black hole…? Let's sit with it for a bit. Let's all
get our breath back. And THEN…*)

ALICE. The policeman takes my name and address.
    He asks what I was doing.
    It's a tough question, so I shrug, he sighs…
    Says they'll be in touch,
    But I seem like a nice girl
    And frankly, they have bigger fish to fry.

    I leave the Town Hall and to be honest
    I don't know what to do.
    I could go home…
    I don't feel ready for Mum and Dad…
    I could go to school,
    But the exam will be over –
    So I walk to St Peter's Square
    Sit on a bench outside the library
    And watch the trams come and go.

    I sit there for ages.
    Hours, maybe. I don't know how long.
    And I try – *really* try –
    To take it all in.

    (*Pause.*)

    The world is unbearable.
    The sky is huge
    And blue
    And beautiful
    And pumped full
    Of toxic chemicals
    And bad dreams
    And everything wrong is massive
    And everything good is tainted

But it doesn't have to be.
Right? It doesn't have to be...

There are boys skateboarding
By the statue of Emmeline Pankhurst
The sun is warm on my face and...

I can hear someone crying.

(ALICE *looks around – finds* CHARLIE *sat nearby.*)

Hi... Sorry. Are you okay?

They turn round, face wet with tears.

Where are your shoes?

They look surprised. Like they'd forgotten they had feet.

CHARLIE. *There was a fire next door. We had to leave. I must've walked.*

ALICE. *Shit. I mean, sorry, that sounds really...*

They're shivering. I think maybe they're in shock, so I ask if they need me to call someone, they say –

CHARLIE. *I tried to disappear... Didn't work.*

ALICE. They look sad... I want to help, but I don't know what to... I'm only...

Nothing seems to be working.

And they smile at that.
Not like a happy smile, more like a... 'Yeah, I get it,' sort of smile...
And that makes me feel... Good.
They say –

CHARLIE. *This is real, isn't it? This is really happening?*

ALICE. I sit beside them.
Think so. Feels it.

And we stay there for just a bit longer.
Like, knees touching,

Not talking just…
Letting it all sink in.
And yeah, it's like *really weird,*
But it's also sort of like – nice, too, y'know?

I turn on my phone.
And I have twenty texts from Mum:
You didn't show at school?
Sweetheart, where are you?
I love you. Please call.

And one from an unknown number –

⁺✦ ALL SENSATION IS APPROPRIATE ⁺✦

And out the corner of my eye
I can see light… Rainbows,
Dancing on the pavement
Round cigarette butts
And little shards of glass.
And somewhere far away…
There's music.

(*Pause.*)

The stranger takes my hand.
Their skin is cool and soft and
We are sat in Manchester City Centre
It's a bright, sunny afternoon
The whole world is at our feet
And we're about to do something –

(*Darkness. That's it.*

The END!

…*Honest. You can go now.*

Go on then.)

A Nick Hern Book

Peak Stuff first published in Great Britain as a paperback original in 2024 by Nick Hern Books Limited, The Glasshouse, 49a Goldhawk Road, London W12 8QP, in association with ThickSkin

Peak Stuff copyright © 2024 Billie Collins

Billie Collins has asserted their right to be identified as the author of this work

Cover design by Rebecca Pitt

Designed and typeset by Nick Hern Books, London
Printed in Great Britain by Mimeo Ltd, Huntingdon, Cambridgeshire PE29 6XX

A CIP catalogue record for this book is available from the British Library

ISBN 978 1 83904 322 2

www.nickhernbooks.co.uk/environmental-policy